PERE FUFEYIN

TECH-SMART GENERATION:

Empowering Digital Natives

Contents

Introduction

In an age where technology weaves its intricate threads into every facet of our lives, the journey of nurturing a Tech-Smart Generation becomes more paramount than ever before. As we draw the final chapter of this enlightening tome to a close, we find ourselves standing at the crossroads of innovation and education, armed with a comprehensive toolkit designed to guide us through the dynamic landscape of the digital era.

The *Tech-Smart School Kits*, the first cornerstone of this trilogy, illuminate the path for educational institutions to seamlessly integrate technology into their pedagogical framework. From creating tech-savvy classrooms to fostering an atmosphere of creativity and innovation, these kits are a guiding light for educators who seek to sculpt a generation of learners prepared to harness the power of the digital realm.

Venturing further, we delve into the **Tech-Smart Teaching Kits**—a treasure trove of strategies, insights, and practices that empower educators to wield digital tools with finesse. Here, the focus is on refining teaching methods, cultivating personalized learning experiences, and nurturing the digital fluency that today's students require to thrive.

Finally, we arrive at the **Tech-Smart Parenting Kits**, an essential resource for guardians and parents navigating the digital landscape alongside their children. From nurturing responsible digital citizenship to striking the delicate balance between screen time and off-screen adventures, these kits equip parents with the wisdom and tools needed to foster a harmonious digital environment at home.

As you journey through these three interlinked volumes, envision the profound impact of their collective wisdom on the future. Imagine a generation of young minds equipped with the skills, knowledge, and ethical framework to stride confidently into the tech-smart world they inherit.

The narrative of the "Tech-Smart Generation: Empowering Digital Natives" trilogy is a testament to the potential that arises when education, teaching, and parenting converge in the digital age. It is an ode to the remarkable transformation that unfolds when innovation and traditional wisdom coalesce, guided by a commitment to nurturing the boundless potential within every digital native.

Dear reader, as you turn the final pages of this book, remember that the journey has only just begun. The path forward is illuminated by the insights, strategies, and inspirations found within the ***Tech-Smart School Kits, Tech-Smart Teaching Kits, and Tech-Smart Parenting Kits.*** Let these volumes be your compass, guiding you toward a future where the digital generation not only adapts to technology but also thrives as its masters.

Embrace this trilogy as a beacon of empowerment, and let its lessons guide you as you shape the destiny of the Tech-Smart Generation—a generation poised to redefine, revolutionize, and reshape the world.

Understanding the Digital Generation: Embracing technology in education

The dawn of the digital generation has ushered in a transformative era in education, one where technology isn't just a supplement but an integral facet of learning. This subtitle delves into the profound shifts that have occurred in educational landscapes worldwide, as educators and institutions embrace technology to enrich and amplify the learning experience. As we navigate this digital realm, we uncover the synergies between traditional pedagogical approaches and innovative technology integration that are shaping the educational landscape of today and tomorrow.

Embracing the Digital Transition:
The integration of technology in education marks a pivotal juncture in modern pedagogy. In this section, we explore the evolving nature of learning, where digital tools and platforms serve as vehicles for engaging and interactive educational experiences. From interactive whiteboards that enliven classroom discussions to online collaboration platforms that transcend geographical boundaries, technology has facilitated a paradigm shift that empowers educators and captivates learners.

Enhanced Engagement and Customized Learning:
Technology transcends the conventional classroom limitations, offering educators an array of tools to create personalized learning journeys. Adaptive learning platforms, for instance, analyze individual learning patterns and tailor content accordingly, ensuring that each student's educational journey aligns with their unique strengths and challenges.

The Global Classroom:
Technology has not only altered the way we learn but has also expanded the classroom's horizons beyond geographical borders. Through virtual

classrooms and online collaborations, students can connect and collaborate with peers and experts worldwide, fostering cross-cultural understanding and preparing them for the interconnected global society.

The Evolution of Resources:

The digital age has revolutionized access to educational resources. Digital libraries, online databases, and multimedia content empower educators to curate dynamic and up-to-date materials that cater to diverse learning styles. This section delves into how the availability of these resources has democratized education and opened doors to a wealth of information previously inaccessible.

Empowering Educators:

The embrace of technology is not solely limited to students—it has become a vital tool for educators as well. Professional development opportunities, online courses, and collaborative platforms enable teachers to continually refine their skills and adapt to the ever-evolving tech-driven educational landscape.

Balancing Tradition and Innovation:

While technology offers an array of opportunities, it's crucial to strike a balance between embracing innovation and preserving the essence of traditional teaching methods. This section explores how the integration of technology respects the values of time-tested educational principles while revolutionizing the delivery and engagement methods.

As we traverse this exploration of technology's role in education, it becomes evident that the digital age offers boundless possibilities for enriching the learning journey. This section encapsulates the transformative power of technology to foster an educational ecosystem where learners thrive, educators innovate, and the boundaries of knowledge extend far beyond what was once imaginable. It sets the stage for a future where technology-driven education isn't merely an option but a necessity to empower the digital generation for the world ahead.

Creating Digital Learning Environments: Integrating digital tools in the classroom

In an age where technology pervades every facet of modern life, education stands at the forefront of digital transformation. This section delves into the profound impact of integrating digital tools within the classroom, ushering in a new era of learning that is dynamic, interactive, and tailored to the needs of today's learners. As educators harness the power of technology, they unveil a realm of possibilities that redefine traditional teaching methods and amplify student engagement.

Empowering Educators as Innovators:
The integration of digital tools empowers educators to transcend the boundaries of traditional teaching. From interactive whiteboards that transform lectures into dynamic discussions to educational apps that gamify learning, technology equips teachers with innovative methods to capture students' attention and foster active participation.

Personalized Learning Journeys:
Digital tools enable educators to create personalized learning experiences that cater to individual learning styles and paces. Adaptive learning platforms analyze students' progress and adapt content to address their strengths and challenges, ensuring a customized learning journey that maximizes comprehension and retention.

Fostering Collaboration and Communication:
Incorporating digital tools doesn't just augment individual learning; it cultivates a culture of collaboration and communication. Online platforms

and interactive apps encourage students to collaborate on projects, share ideas, and engage in peer reviews, reflecting the collaborative nature of today's interconnected world.

Transcending Classroom Boundaries:

One of the most transformative aspects of digital integration is its capacity to transcend classroom walls. Virtual field trips, video conferencing with experts, and accessing global resources online enrich the educational experience by exposing students to diverse perspectives and cultures.

Data-Driven Insights:

Digital tools provide educators with data-driven insights into students' progress and learning patterns. This information equips teachers with the ability to tailor instruction to meet individual needs, thereby ensuring that no student is left behind.

Cultivating Digital Literacy:

As digital natives, students need to cultivate not only subject-specific knowledge but also digital literacy skills. Integrating technology into the classroom not only imparts academic content but also equips students with the ability to navigate the digital landscape responsibly and effectively.

Holistic Assessment Techniques:

Digital tools offer a variety of assessment techniques beyond traditional tests, allowing educators to gauge students' understanding through multimedia projects, interactive quizzes, and collaborative assignments. This diversified approach to assessment captures a more comprehensive view of students' abilities.

As we traverse the landscape of integrating digital tools in the classroom, we uncover a transformative journey that reshapes education for the digital era. This section encapsulates the realization that technology isn't just a supplementary asset; it is a catalyst for a revolution in pedagogy, one that empowers educators to craft dynamic learning environments and propels students towards a future that's informed, connected, and equipped with the skills to thrive in a digital world. With digital integration, education ceases to be confined to textbooks and lecture halls, embracing innovation as it cultivates the leaders of tomorrow.

Cyber Security And Online Safety: Safeguarding Students In The Digital Age

In the ever-expanding realm of the digital landscape, ensuring the safety and security of students has become an imperative. This section delves into the critical subject of cyber security and online safety, highlighting the significance of equipping students with the knowledge and skills to navigate the digital world responsibly and securely. As the digital age ushers in unprecedented opportunities, it also presents an array of risks that demand our attention, vigilance, and proactive measures.

The Digital Frontier:
The integration of technology into education has opened doors to boundless resources and avenues for learning. However, this exposure also brings forth challenges, with cyber threats and online dangers lurking in the digital shadows.

Understanding Cyber security:
This section unravels the intricacies of cyber security, delving into the various forms of online threats that students may encounter. From phishing attacks to malware, understanding these threats is the first step towards fortifying our students' digital defenses.

Promoting Digital Literacy:

Empowering students with digital literacy skills is akin to arming them with shields against the digital dangers that persist. Educating them about identifying suspicious links, verifying sources, and practicing responsible online behavior is crucial for their safety.

Navigating the Perils of Social Media:

Social media platforms offer opportunities for connection and self-expression, but they also come with potential pitfalls such as cyber bullying, oversharing of personal information, and exposure to inappropriate content. This section addresses the importance of guiding students in making informed choices when navigating the social media landscape.

Online Etiquette and Respectful Behavior:

The digital realm mirrors the real world in its demand for courtesy and respect. This section emphasizes the significance of instilling in students the values of empathy, respect, and ethical behavior, both online and offline.

Privacy Protection:

As students engage with digital platforms, their personal information becomes vulnerable. Educating them about the importance of protecting their privacy and using strong passwords is essential for maintaining their digital security.

Educator and Parent Roles:

In a collaborative effort, educators and parents play a pivotal role in equipping students with the skills to remain safe online. This section delves into how open communication between schools and families can create a united front against online threats.

As we navigate this exploration of cyber security and online safety, it becomes evident that safeguarding students in the digital age is not only a responsibility but a collective commitment. This section encapsulates the urgency of fostering a digital environment that prioritizes the well-being of students, arming them with knowledge, critical thinking skills, and a profound sense of responsibility. Just as we teach them to safely cross the road, we must guide them to navigate the digital highway, ensuring their journey is secure, enlightening, and empowering. With cyber safety education, we lay the foundation for students to emerge as informed digital citizens who traverse the digital realm with confidence, resilience, and the ability to thrive in a digital world while upholding their safety and dignity.

Leveraging Edtech: Enhancing Teaching And Learning Experiences

In the dynamic landscape of education, technology has emerged as a powerful catalyst for transforming teaching and learning experiences. This section delves into the realm of Educational Technology (EdTech), unveiling its potential to reshape classrooms, redefine pedagogies, and foster an environment where students and educators alike thrive. As technology becomes an integral part of the educational ecosystem, educators are presented with innovative tools that amplify engagement, encourage collaboration, and unlock new dimensions of learning.

Empowering Educators:

EdTech serves as a toolbox that equips educators with a diverse array of tools to create engaging and interactive lessons. From interactive whiteboards that bring lessons to life to learning management systems that streamline administrative tasks, technology empowers educators to maximize their impact.

Personalized Learning Journeys:

One of the defining features of EdTech is its capacity to facilitate personalized learning experiences. Adaptive learning platforms analyze students' progress and adapt content to meet individual needs, allowing each student to learn at their own pace and in a way that suits their learning style.

Interactive and Engaging Content:
EdTech breathes life into learning materials, transforming them from static text to interactive experiences. Multimedia elements, simulations, and virtual reality content engage students' senses and make learning both immersive and captivating.

Global Collaboration:
EdTech transcends geographical barriers, enabling students to collaborate with peers from around the world. Virtual classrooms, online discussion forums, and collaborative project platforms foster cross-cultural interactions, enhancing students' global awareness and communication skills.

Data-Driven Insights:
EdTech provides educators with valuable insights into students' progress, strengths, and areas that need improvement. This data-driven approach informs instructional strategies and enables educators to provide timely interventions to ensure student success.

Inclusive Education:
EdTech has the power to level the playing field for students with diverse learning needs. Accessibility features, such as text-to-speech and closed captioning, ensure that all students can access and engage with the content.

Professional Development and Growth:
EdTech isn't just a tool for students—it's also a resource for educators to continually enhance their skills. Online courses, webinars, and collaborative networks enable teachers to stay updated with the latest trends and best practices in education.

As we navigate the landscape of EdTech, it becomes evident that its integration isn't a mere trend but a fundamental shift in the way education is experienced and delivered. This section encapsulates the transformative power of EdTech to revolutionize traditional classrooms into hubs of exploration, innovation, and collaboration. It underscores the notion that technology isn't replacing educators but enhancing their role, allowing them to unleash their creativity and deliver impactful learning experiences. With EdTech, education is no longer confined to the boundaries of the physical classroom—it extends to a digital realm where limitless opportunities await, where students become active learners and educators evolve into facilitators of discovery. As we embrace EdTech, we embark on an educational odyssey that empowers learners, ignites curiosity, and equips the next generation to thrive in a rapidly evolving world.

1

1

Tech-Smart School Toolkit: Practical Guide for Digital Natives

I n a world where technology evolves at lightning speed, preparing the next generation for the digital landscape is not just a choice – it's an imperative. *Tech-Smart Generation: Empowering Digital Natives* is more than just a book; it's a transformative guide that navigates the intersection of education and technology, equipping educators, parents, and students with the tools they need to thrive in the digital era.

This captivating and forward-looking book delves into the heart of the digital native experience, offering insights into harnessing the potential of technology while mitigating its risks. The authors, renowned experts in education and technology, have crafted a comprehensive roadmap for creating a Tech-Smart School Toolkit. This toolkit isn't just theoretical; it's a pragmatic and actionable guide that educators can implement right away. It provides innovative teaching methodologies, adaptable curriculum frameworks, and strategies for fostering digital citizenship and well-being.

Tech-Smart Generation doesn't just stop at classroom strategies. It delves into the roles of parents and guardians, helping them understand and navigate the complex digital landscape their children inhabit. From screen time management to promoting healthy online behaviors, this book empowers adults to become effective guides in their children's digital journeys.

The book's empowering narrative is supported by real-life case studies, cutting-edge research, and practical exercises that bridge the gap between theory and application. Whether you're an educator seeking to create an engaging tech-integrated classroom, a parent striving to strike a balance between online and offline worlds, or a student eager to leverage technology for growth, this book offers a rich toolbox of ideas.

"Tech-Smart Generation: Empowering Digital Natives" isn't just a book; it's a guiding light for embracing technology as a powerful educational ally. It's a call to action, a beacon of hope, and a manual for ensuring that the digital natives of today become the empowered leaders of tomorrow.

Understanding The Digital Generation: Embracing Technology In Education

The dawn of the digital generation has ushered in a transformative era in education, one where technology isn't just a supplement but an integral facet of learning. This subtitle delves into the profound shifts that have occurred in educational landscapes worldwide, as educators and institutions embrace technology to enrich and amplify the learning experience. As we navigate this digital realm, we uncover the synergies between traditional pedagogical approaches and innovative technology integration that are shaping the educational landscape of today and tomorrow.

Embracing the Digital Transition:

The integration of technology in education marks a pivotal juncture in modern pedagogy. In this section, we explore the evolving nature of learning, where digital tools and platforms serve as vehicles for engaging and interactive educational experiences. From interactive whiteboards that enliven classroom discussions to online collaboration platforms that transcend geographical boundaries, technology has facilitated a paradigm shift that empowers educators and captivates learners.

Enhanced Engagement and Customized Learning:

Technology transcends the conventional classroom limitations, offering educators an array of tools to create personalized learning journeys. Adaptive learning platforms, for instance, analyze individual learning patterns and tailor content accordingly, ensuring that each student's educational journey aligns with their unique strengths and challenges.

The Global Classroom:

Technology has not only altered the way we learn but has also expanded the classroom's horizons beyond geographical borders. Through virtual classrooms and online collaborations, students can connect and collaborate with peers and experts worldwide, fostering cross-cultural understanding and preparing them for the interconnected global society.

The Evolution of Resources:

The digital age has revolutionized access to educational resources. Digital libraries, online databases, and multimedia content empower educators to curate dynamic and up-to-date materials that cater to diverse learning styles. This section delves into how the availability of these resources has democratized education and opened doors to a wealth of information previously inaccessible.

Empowering Educators:

The embrace of technology is not solely limited to students—it has become a vital tool for educators as well. Professional development opportunities, online courses, and collaborative platforms enable teachers to continually refine their skills and adapt to the ever-evolving tech-driven educational landscape.

Balancing Tradition and Innovation:
While technology offers an array of opportunities, it's crucial to strike a balance between embracing innovation and preserving the essence of traditional teaching methods. This section explores how the integration of technology respects the values of time-tested educational principles while revolutionizing the delivery and engagement methods.

As we traverse this exploration of technology's role in education, it becomes evident that the digital age offers boundless possibilities for enriching the learning journey. This section encapsulates the transformative power of technology to foster an educational ecosystem where learners thrive, educators innovate, and the boundaries of knowledge extend far beyond what was once imaginable. It sets the stage for a future where technology-driven education isn't merely an option but a necessity to empower the digital generation for the world ahead.

Creating Digital Learning Environments: Integrating digital tools in the classroom

In an age where technology pervades every facet of modern life, education stands at the forefront of digital transformation. This section delves into the profound impact of integrating digital tools within the classroom, ushering in a new era of learning that is dynamic, interactive, and tailored to the needs of today's learners. As educators harness the power of technology, they unveil a realm of possibilities that redefine traditional teaching methods and amplify student engagement.

Empowering Educators as Innovators:
The integration of digital tools empowers educators to transcend the boundaries of traditional teaching. From interactive whiteboards that transform lectures into dynamic discussions to educational apps that gamify learning, technology equips teachers with innovative methods to capture students' attention and foster active participation.

Personalized Learning Journeys:
Digital tools enable educators to create personalized learning experiences that cater to individual learning styles and paces. Adaptive learning platforms analyze students' progress and adapt content to address their strengths and challenges, ensuring a customized learning journey that maximizes comprehension and retention.

Fostering Collaboration and Communication:
Incorporating digital tools doesn't just augment individual learning; it cultivates a culture of collaboration and communication. Online platforms and interactive apps encourage students to collaborate on projects, share ideas, and engage in peer reviews, reflecting the collaborative nature of today's

interconnected world.

Transcending Classroom Boundaries:
One of the most transformative aspects of digital integration is its capacity to transcend classroom walls. Virtual field trips, video conferencing with experts, and accessing global resources online enrich the educational experience by exposing students to diverse perspectives and cultures.

Data-Driven Insights:
Digital tools provide educators with data-driven insights into students' progress and learning patterns. This information equips teachers with the ability to tailor instruction to meet individual needs, thereby ensuring that no student is left behind.

Cultivating Digital Literacy:
As digital natives, students need to cultivate not only subject-specific knowledge but also digital literacy skills. Integrating technology into the classroom not only imparts academic content but also equips students with the ability to navigate the digital landscape responsibly and effectively.

Holistic Assessment Techniques:
Digital tools offer a variety of assessment techniques beyond traditional tests, allowing educators to gauge students' understanding through multimedia projects, interactive quizzes, and collaborative assignments. This diversified approach to assessment captures a more comprehensive view of students' abilities.

As we traverse the landscape of integrating digital tools in the classroom, we uncover a transformative journey that reshapes education for the digital era. This section encapsulates the realization that technology isn't just a supplementary asset; it is a catalyst for a revolution in pedagogy, one that empowers educators to craft dynamic learning environments and propels students towards a future that's informed, connected, and equipped with the skills to thrive in a digital world. With digital integration, education ceases to be confined to textbooks and lecture halls, embracing innovation as it cultivates the leaders of tomorrow.

Cyber Security And Online Safety: Safeguarding Students In The Digital Age

In the ever-expanding realm of the digital landscape, ensuring the safety and security of students has become an imperative. This section delves into the critical subject of cyber security and online safety, highlighting the significance of equipping students with the knowledge and skills to navigate the digital world responsibly and securely. As the digital age ushers in unprecedented opportunities, it also presents an array of risks that demand our attention, vigilance, and proactive measures.

The Digital Frontier:
   The integration of technology into education has opened doors to boundless resources and avenues for learning. However, this exposure also brings forth challenges, with cyber threats and online dangers lurking in the digital shadows.

Understanding Cyber security:
   This section unravels the intricacies of cyber security, delving into the various forms of online threats that students may encounter. From phishing attacks to malware, understanding these threats is the first step towards fortifying our students' digital defenses.

Promoting Digital Literacy:
   Empowering students with digital literacy skills is akin to arming them

with shields against the digital dangers that persist. Educating them about identifying suspicious links, verifying sources, and practicing responsible online behavior is crucial for their safety.

Navigating the Perils of Social Media:

Social media platforms offer opportunities for connection and self-expression, but they also come with potential pitfalls such as cyber bullying, oversharing of personal information, and exposure to inappropriate content. This section addresses the importance of guiding students in making informed choices when navigating the social media landscape.

Online Etiquette and Respectful Behavior:

The digital realm mirrors the real world in its demand for courtesy and respect. This section emphasizes the significance of instilling in students the values of empathy, respect, and ethical behavior, both online and offline.

Privacy Protection:

As students engage with digital platforms, their personal information becomes vulnerable. Educating them about the importance of protecting their privacy and using strong passwords is essential for maintaining their digital security.

Educator and Parent Roles:

In a collaborative effort, educators and parents play a pivotal role in equipping students with the skills to remain safe online. This section delves into how open communication between schools and families can create a united front against online threats.

As we navigate this exploration of cyber security and online safety, it becomes evident that safeguarding students in the digital age is not only a responsibility but a collective commitment. This section encapsulates the urgency of fostering a digital environment that prioritizes the well-being of students, arming them with knowledge, critical thinking skills, and a profound sense of responsibility. Just as we teach them to safely cross the road, we must guide them to navigate the digital highway, ensuring their journey is secure, enlightening, and empowering. With cyber safety education, we lay the foundation for students to emerge as informed digital citizens who traverse the digital realm with confidence, resilience, and the ability to thrive in a digital world while upholding their safety and dignity.

Leveraging Edtech: Enhancing Teaching And Learning Experiences

In the dynamic landscape of education, technology has emerged as a powerful catalyst for transforming teaching and learning experiences. This section delves into the realm of Educational Technology (EdTech), unveiling its potential to reshape classrooms, redefine pedagogies, and foster an environment where students and educators alike thrive. As technology becomes an integral part of the educational ecosystem, educators are presented with innovative tools that amplify engagement, encourage collaboration, and unlock new dimensions of learning.

Empowering Educators:

EdTech serves as a toolbox that equips educators with a diverse array of tools to create engaging and interactive lessons. From interactive whiteboards that bring lessons to life to learning management systems that streamline administrative tasks, technology empowers educators to maximize their impact.

Personalized Learning Journeys:

One of the defining features of EdTech is its capacity to facilitate personalized learning experiences. Adaptive learning platforms analyze students' progress and adapt content to meet individual needs, allowing each student to learn at their own pace and in a way that suits their learning style.

Interactive and Engaging Content:

EdTech breathes life into learning materials, transforming them from static text to interactive experiences. Multimedia elements, simulations, and virtual reality content engage students' senses and make learning both immersive and captivating.

Global Collaboration:

EdTech transcends geographical barriers, enabling students to collaborate with peers from around the world. Virtual classrooms, online discussion forums, and collaborative project platforms foster cross-cultural interactions, enhancing students' global awareness and communication skills.

Data-Driven Insights:

EdTech provides educators with valuable insights into students' progress, strengths, and areas that need improvement. This data-driven approach informs instructional strategies and enables educators to provide timely interventions to ensure student success.

Inclusive Education:

EdTech has the power to level the playing field for students with diverse learning needs. Accessibility features, such as text-to-speech and closed captioning, ensure that all students can access and engage with the content.

Professional Development and Growth:

EdTech isn't just a tool for students—it's also a resource for educators to continually enhance their skills. Online courses, webinars, and collaborative networks enable teachers to stay updated with the latest trends and best practices in education.

As we navigate the landscape of EdTech, it becomes evident that its integration isn't a mere trend but a fundamental shift in the way education is experienced and delivered. This section encapsulates the transformative power of EdTech to revolutionize traditional classrooms into hubs of exploration, innovation, and collaboration. It underscores the notion that technology isn't replacing educators but enhancing their role, allowing them to unleash their creativity and deliver impactful learning experiences. With EdTech, education is no longer confined to the boundaries of the physical classroom—it extends to a digital realm where limitless opportunities await, where students become active learners and educators evolve into facilitators of discovery. As we embrace EdTech, we embark on an educational odyssey that empowers learners, ignites curiosity, and equips the next generation to thrive in a rapidly evolving world.

2

Tech-Smart Teaching Toolkit: Practical Guide for Digital Natives

The "Tech-Smart Teaching Toolkit: Practical Guide for Digital Natives" is an indispensable compass for educators navigating the uncharted waters of modern education. This comprehensive guide unfurls a captivating journey into the realm of teaching in the digital age, where traditional chalkboards meet cutting-edge technology, and pedagogy fuses seamlessly with innovation.

In a world where digital natives are born with smartphones in hand and coding as a second language, this toolkit is a treasure trove of insights, strategies, and actionable steps to bridge the gap between the classroom and the digital domain. It's not just a manual; it's a dynamic playbook that empowers educators to harness the transformative potential of technology, while nurturing the unique strengths and challenges that come with a tech-savvy generation.

From creating engaging digital learning environments to fostering digital citizenship, this guide navigates every twist and turn of the educational journey, turning challenges into opportunities and uncertainties into triumphs. It's a roadmap that champions adaptability, creativity, and a deep understanding of the pulse of digital natives.

As you leaf through its pages, you'll uncover a wealth of wisdom from seasoned educators and technologists, leading you to the crossroads of innovation and tradition. From deciphering the nuances of digital fluency to balancing screen time, this toolkit arms you with the tools to cultivate a generation of learners who are not just tech-consumers, but tech-creators, ready to navigate the complex landscape of the future.

In a world where education is at a crossroads of analog and digital, the "Tech-Smart Teaching Toolkit" stands as a guiding light, offering educators the keys to unlocking the potential of a new era of learning. Whether you're a seasoned educator looking to infuse your teaching with tech-savviness or a novice teacher taking your first steps into this brave new world, this guide is your steadfast companion—a beacon of inspiration and practicality that propels you toward nurturing the digital natives of today into the trailblazers of tomorrow.

Nurturing Digital Literacy: Equipping educators with digital skills

In an age where digital technology permeates every facet of our lives, nurturing digital literacy has become an essential mission in education. The "Nurturing Digital Literacy" section of the "Tech-Smart Teaching Toolkit" is a profound exploration into the world of equipping educators with the necessary skills to navigate the digital landscape. This chapter is not just about understanding the ins and outs of gadgets and software—it's about empowering educators to be confident leaders in a rapidly evolving digital age.

The Digital Frontier:

Digital literacy is no longer a niche skill—it's a fundamental competency that empowers educators to enrich their teaching methodologies and enhance student engagement. This section introduces the concept of digital literacy as a multifaceted skill set that goes beyond technical prowess. It's about understanding how to harness technology for effective communication, critical thinking, problem-solving, and innovation.

Navigating the Digital Landscape:

As educators embark on the journey of digital literacy, they discover a diverse array of tools at their disposal. From understanding cloud computing to embracing online collaboration platforms, this section dives into the various facets of the digital realm that educators need to master.

Data Literacy and Analysis:

In a world driven by data, educators must possess the ability to decipher and interpret information to make informed decisions. Digital literacy extends to understanding data analytics, enabling educators to glean insights that inform instructional strategies and drive student success.

Digital Citizenship and Ethics:

As digital role models, educators play a pivotal role in shaping responsible digital citizens. This section delves into topics such as online etiquette, privacy protection, and the ethical use of technology—a crucial aspect of digital literacy that educators must instill in their students.

Tech Integration in Pedagogy:

Digital literacy isn't just about knowing how to use technology—it's about seamlessly integrating it into pedagogical practices. This section explores the intersection of digital literacy and effective teaching methods, highlighting how educators can leverage technology to create engaging and dynamic learning experiences.

Continuous Learning and Growth:

The digital landscape is in constant flux, demanding educators to be perpetual learners. From online courses to professional learning networks, this section emphasizes the importance of ongoing growth in digital literacy, empowering educators to stay ahead in an ever-changing digital world.

As educators immerse themselves in the world of digital literacy, they embark on a transformative journey that transcends the boundaries of the classroom. This section encapsulates the notion that nurturing digital literacy isn't just about learning to use digital tools—it's about cultivating a mindset of adaptability, curiosity, and resilience. As educators become proficient in digital literacy, they become torchbearers, lighting the path for their students and inspiring them to be confident, capable, and responsible digital citizens. The "Nurturing Digital Literacy" chapter is a call to action, inviting educators to embrace their role as digital guides, equipping themselves with the skills that empower them to lead their students into a future where technology is not just a tool, but a key to unlocking endless possibilities.

Interactive Classroom Strategies: Engaging Students Through Technology

The landscape of education has undergone a profound transformation with the integration of technology into classrooms. The "Interactive Classroom Strategies" section within the "Tech-Smart Teaching Toolkit" is a dynamic exploration into the realm of engaging students through innovative technological approaches. This chapter isn't just about using devices—it's about leveraging technology to create immersive, collaborative, and student-centered learning experiences.

Shifting from Passive to Active Learning:

In traditional classrooms, students often assume passive roles as recipients of information. This section introduces a paradigm shift, emphasizing interactive strategies that transform students into active participants in their own learning journey. With the integration of technology, educators have the tools to make lessons come alive and engage students on a deeper level.

Gamification and Learning Games:

Gamification harnesses the innate human inclination for competition and rewards to enhance learning experiences. This section delves into the integration of game-like elements into lessons, fostering engagement, healthy competition, and a sense of accomplishment among students.

Flipped Classroom Models:

Technology enables educators to flip the traditional classroom model, where students access instructional content online before class and engage in collaborative activities during class time. This strategy fosters deeper understanding, critical thinking, and peer interaction.

Collaborative Platforms and Tools:

The digital era has redefined collaboration, enabling students to work together regardless of physical boundaries. From virtual whiteboards to cloud-based document sharing, this section explores the myriad ways technology facilitates collaborative projects and group activities.

Interactive Presentations and Polling:

Static presentations are transformed into dynamic experiences through interactive tools. Educators can engage students by integrating polls, quizzes, and interactive elements that promote active participation and real-time feedback.

Augmented and Virtual Reality:

Immersive technologies like augmented and virtual reality transport students into vivid learning environments. This section delves into their potential to enhance subjects like science, history, and even art by allowing students to explore concepts in a tangible way.

Multimedia Projects and Digital Storytelling:
Technology enables students to express their creativity through multimedia projects and digital storytelling. This section highlights the power of visual and auditory mediums to convey information and ideas effectively.

Empowering Diverse Learning Styles:
Every student learns differently. With technology, educators can cater to diverse learning styles—visual, auditory, kinesthetic, and more—ensuring that all students are engaged and can absorb content in a way that resonates with them.

The "Interactive Classroom Strategies" chapter underscores the transformative power of technology in shaping the classroom of the future. It's a call to action for educators to step beyond the boundaries of traditional teaching methods and embrace interactive approaches that spark curiosity, stimulate critical thinking, and foster a lifelong love for learning. As technology seamlessly weaves into the fabric of education, the classroom transcends its physical confines, becoming a hub of exploration, creativity, and collaboration. Through interactive strategies, educators are not just teaching content—they're cultivating a generation of agile thinkers, problem-solvers, and innovators who are poised to thrive in a world where adaptability and technological fluency are paramount.

Gamification and Edutainment: Enhancing learning outcomes with fun activities

Education, once confined to traditional textbooks and lectures, has undergone a remarkable transformation in the digital age. The "Gamification and Edutainment" section of the "Tech-Smart Teaching Toolkit" delves into a realm where learning meets play, where engagement meets entertainment, and where education becomes an immersive adventure.

The Gamification Revolution:
Gamification is a pedagogical approach that harnesses the principles of games to enhance learning experiences. This section unveils the power of turning educational content into captivating challenges, quests, and competitions. By introducing elements such as rewards, points, and leaderboards, educators can inspire healthy competition, intrinsic motivation, and a zest for mastering complex concepts.

Edutainment as Learning Catalyst:
Edutainment, the fusion of education and entertainment, is a catalyst for engagement. This section explores how educators can infuse lessons with elements of storytelling, humor, and creativity to captivate students' attention and cultivate a passion for learning.

Creating Immersive Learning Environments:
Imagine exploring ancient civilizations, delving into the cosmos, or dissecting virtual organisms—all within the classroom. Gamification and edutainment enable educators to create immersive learning environments that transport students beyond the confines of textbooks.

Engaging with Digital Storytelling:
Stories have been an intrinsic part of human culture for centuries. This section showcases how educators can leverage digital storytelling to weave

narratives that contextualize subjects, make learning relatable, and kindle students' curiosity.

Championing Critical Thinking and Problem-Solving:
Games are often designed with intricate challenges that require strategic thinking and problem-solving. This section delves into how gamification fosters these skills, as students grapple with scenarios that demand analytical thought and creative solutions.

Personalized Learning Journeys:
One size does not fit all in education. Gamification and edutainment allow for personalized learning paths, where students can progress at their own pace and delve deeper into areas of interest.

Gamified Assessments and Evaluation:
Traditional assessments can feel mundane, but gamification breathes new life into evaluation methods. This section explores how quizzes, puzzles, and interactive challenges transform assessment into an engaging experience that gauges true understanding.

Fostering Intrinsic Motivation:
Intrinsic motivation, the drive that comes from within, is a cornerstone of effective learning. Gamification taps into this by making learning inherently rewarding, ensuring that students actively seek knowledge out of genuine curiosity.

The "Gamification and Edutainment" chapter isn't just about adding a fun veneer to education—it's about changing the way students perceive learning. By infusing lessons with elements of gamification and edutainment, educators cultivate a mindset where learning is not a chore, but an exhilarating adventure. As students engage in challenges, unravel mysteries, and explore virtual realms, they're developing skills that extend far beyond the classroom—skills like critical thinking, collaboration, resilience, and adaptability. Gamification and edutainment are the keys to nurturing a generation of lifelong learners, individuals who are not just absorbing information, but actively seeking it, driven by a passion for knowledge that will propel them into a future defined by constant innovation and growth.

Assessing Digital Progress: Measuring Success In The Tech-Savvy Era

The integration of technology in education has ushered in a new era of teaching and learning, one that is dynamic, interactive, and constantly evolving. In the "Assessing Digital Progress" section of the "Tech-Smart Teaching Toolkit," educators are equipped with the tools and strategies to effectively gauge the impact of technology on student learning and measure success in this rapidly changing landscape.

Navigating the Digital Assessment Landscape:
   Traditional methods of assessment are no longer sufficient in a tech-savvy era. This section delves into the diverse range of assessment approaches, from formative assessments that provide real-time insights into student understanding to summative assessments that capture overall achievement.

Data-Driven Decision Making:
   With the integration of technology, educators have access to a wealth of data that can inform instructional strategies. This section explores how data analytics and educational technology platforms can be leveraged to gain actionable insights that guide teaching practices and enhance learning outcomes.

Evaluating Digital Literacy and Fluency:
   In a world dominated by digital tools, assessing students' digital literacy and

fluency is crucial. This section delves into strategies for evaluating students' ability to navigate and utilize technology effectively, ensuring they are well-equipped for the demands of the modern world.

Measuring Collaborative Skills:

Technology enables seamless collaboration, transcending geographical barriers. This section explores assessment methods that gauge students' ability to collaborate effectively in virtual environments, fostering teamwork and communication skills that are essential in the digital age.

Assessing Critical Thinking and Problem-Solving:

As students engage with interactive digital content, their critical thinking and problem-solving skills are constantly challenged. This section delves into assessment approaches that capture these skills, from analyzing students' ability to dissect complex problems to evaluating their capacity to synthesize information from various digital sources.

Incorporating Authentic Assessment:

Authentic assessments mirror real-world scenarios, providing a holistic view of students' skills. This section explores project-based assessments, presentations, and portfolio evaluations that showcase students' ability to apply their digital skills to practical situations.

Balancing Quantitative and Qualitative Assessment:

Technology provides an array of quantitative data, but qualitative assessment is equally important. This section discusses strategies for incorporating both types of assessment to provide a comprehensive understanding of students' progress.

Ethical and Responsible Tech Use Assessment:

In the digital era, ethical tech use is paramount. This section addresses the assessment of students' ability to navigate the digital landscape responsibly, emphasizing aspects like online etiquette, data privacy, and responsible content consumption.

The "Assessing Digital Progress" chapter underscores the transformative potential of technology in redefining assessment practices. As educators navigate the challenges and opportunities of the tech-savvy era, they have the power to not only measure academic achievement but also nurture skills that prepare students for success in an increasingly digital world. By embracing diverse assessment approaches, educators ensure that their teaching is aligned with the needs of the modern learner, fostering adaptable, critically thinking, and tech-savvy individuals who are poised to thrive in the ever-evolving landscape of the 21st century.

3

Tech-Smart Parenting Toolkit: Practical Guide for Digital Natives

In a world where screens seem to seamlessly merge with daily life, parenting has taken on a new dimension—one where touchscreens are as common as teddy bears, and digital footprints accompany every step. Welcome to the "Tech-Smart Parenting Toolkit," where the journey of raising digital natives is illuminated with insights, strategies, and a touch of magic.

Parenting in the digital age presents both awe-inspiring opportunities and bewildering challenges. As we marvel at how effortlessly our children navigate apps and interfaces, we're also faced with questions about screen time, online safety, and the ever-elusive balance between virtual and tangible experiences. This toolkit is a guiding compass, designed to empower parents as they navigate this brave new world alongside their tech-savvy offspring.

In this digital realm, toddlers seem to grasp smartphones with the same ease as building blocks. Adolescents navigate complex online spaces, where friendship, learning, and self-expression intertwine. As parents, how do we provide guidance in this unfamiliar terrain? How do we foster healthy relationships with screens while nurturing offline connections?

From understanding the nuances of digital citizenship to discovering the art of tech-smart parenting, this toolkit unravels the mysteries of modern parenthood. It's not about resisting the digital tide; it's about riding it skillfully. It's about shaping the digital experiences of our children while safeguarding their well-being, ensuring that they emerge from their screens as curious explorers and responsible citizens.

In the following chapters, we'll explore the tools to navigate this journey. We'll delve into fostering healthy tech habits, nurturing digital literacy, and fostering open dialogues that bridge the generational tech gap. We'll discover the world of educational apps and platforms, unlock the secrets of cyber etiquette, and uncover ways to balance screen time with real-world adventures.

The "Tech-Smart Parenting Toolkit" isn't just about surviving in the digital age—it's about thriving in it. It's about embracing the potential of technology while grounding our parenting in timeless values. It's about recognizing that we are the guides, the navigators, and the storytellers of our children's digital narratives.

So, whether you're a digital immigrant adapting to this new age or a digital native raising the next generation, join us on this captivating journey. Let's empower ourselves with knowledge, wisdom, and a dash of tech-savvy magic as we navigate the uncharted waters of tech-smart parenting. Welcome to a toolkit that illuminates the path toward raising resilient, responsible, and truly tech-smart digital natives.

Empowering Digital Parenting: Navigating the digital landscape together

In an era where children seem to be born with smartphones in hand and tablets at their fingertips, the journey of parenthood has taken an exciting twist. The "Empowering Digital Parenting" chapter of the "Tech-Smart Parenting Toolkit" is your steadfast companion as you navigate this uncharted terrain, offering insights, strategies, and a guiding light to raise confident, resilient digital natives.

Digital Fluency: A New Language for Parents:
Just as children learn languages effortlessly, they also become fluent in the language of technology from an early age. As parents, our role transcends that of mere spectators; we become co-pilots in their digital adventures. This chapter guides us in embracing this shared journey, ensuring we're equipped to understand and engage with their tech-savvy world.

Bridging the Generational Gap:
The gap between digital natives and digital immigrants (that's us!) can sometimes feel like a vast chasm. This chapter serves as a bridge, offering insights into the digital experiences that shape our children's lives. By understanding their digital landscape, we can initiate meaningful conversations that bridge generations and foster mutual understanding.

Crafting Digital House Rules:
Every household has its own set of rules, values, and rhythms. As technology seamlessly integrates into our lives, it's crucial to craft digital house rules that align with our family's dynamics. This chapter offers practical guidance on setting screen-time limits, designing tech-free zones, and cultivating a balanced approach to digital engagement.

Parental Controls: A Digital Safety Net:
As our children navigate the online world, our role as protectors takes on a digital dimension. This chapter equips us with the knowledge and tools to

implement effective parental controls. From filtering content to monitoring online activity, we ensure a safer online experience without stifling their exploration.

The Power of Tech-Smart Communication:
The digital age has transformed the way we communicate. Our children engage with emojis, memes, and social media platforms that can sometimes feel like an enigma. This chapter uncovers the secrets of tech-savvy communication, helping us decode the nuances of their digital conversations while nurturing open lines of dialogue.

Digital Literacy Starts at Home:
Just as we teach our children to read, write, and count, digital literacy is an essential skill for the modern age. This chapter guides us in nurturing their digital literacy, from discerning credible sources to understanding online privacy and ethical digital behavior.

Modeling Responsible Tech Use:
Children learn by example, and our tech habits set the tone for their own digital behavior. This chapter encourages us to reflect on our tech habits, demonstrating the responsible use of technology while demonstrating the importance of unplugging and connecting with the real world.

Celebrating Digital Moments:
Technology offers a canvas for creativity and self-expression. From sharing digital artwork to capturing fleeting moments, this chapter explores ways to celebrate our children's digital achievements while cherishing the precious moments that unfold both on and offline.

As we embrace the role of digital parents, this chapter reinforces the essence of our journey: empowerment. We hold the tools to raise tech-savvy children who are equipped to thrive in a rapidly evolving world. By navigating the digital landscape together, we create a harmonious blend of technology and human connection, ensuring our children embark on their digital adventures with curiosity, confidence, and resilience.

Digital Well-Being: Balancing Screen Time And Healthy Habits

In the ever-evolving landscape of parenting, the concept of well-being has taken on a new dimension: digital well-being. The chapter on "Digital Well-being: Balancing Screen Time and Healthy Habits" in the "Tech-Smart Parenting Toolkit" invites parents to embark on a journey of fostering a harmonious relationship between technology and wellness, ensuring that our digital natives thrive in both virtual and real environments.

Navigating the Digital Maze:

As screens become an integral part of our children's lives, striking a balance between screen time and other activities is more critical than ever. This chapter acts as a compass, guiding us through the maze of digital interactions and illuminating the path toward a healthier screen-time routine.

The Digital Diet: Nutritious Screen Time:

Just as a balanced diet nourishes our bodies, a balanced digital diet nourishes our minds. This chapter delves into the idea of nutritious screen time—engaging with content that educates, inspires, and uplifts. By curating meaningful digital experiences, we ensure that every moment spent on screens contributes positively to our children's growth.

Unplugging: Cultivating Offline Adventures:

From virtual realms to real-life adventures, this chapter encourages us to unplug from the digital world and embrace the tangible experiences that life offers. Whether it's outdoor play, art projects, or simply spending quality time together, these moments foster creativity, human connection, and well-rounded development.

Digital Detox: Recharging Through Disconnecting:
Just as devices need charging, our minds and bodies require rejuvenation. The concept of a digital detox is explored, offering practical strategies to periodically disconnect from screens and reconnect with ourselves and our loved ones.

Mindful Screen Time: Presence in the Digital Age:
Mindfulness, a timeless practice, finds a new context in the digital age. This chapter introduces the art of mindful screen time—a practice that encourages being present while engaging with technology. By nurturing this skill, we teach our children to navigate the digital world with intention and awareness.

Sleep Hygiene in the Digital Era:
Screen time and sleep are intertwined in the modern world, with devices often accompanying us to the bedroom. This chapter highlights the significance of sleep hygiene, offering strategies to create a tech-free sleep sanctuary that supports restful nights and productive days.

Tech-Free Zones: Crafting Spaces for Balance:
In a world filled with screens, creating tech-free zones is crucial to preserving the sanctity of certain spaces. From the dining table to the bedroom, this chapter explores the benefits of carving out zones where technology takes a backseat, enabling meaningful face-to-face interactions.

The Joy of Outdoor Adventures:
Nature has a magical ability to heal and invigorate. This chapter extols the virtues of outdoor adventures, whether it's a walk in the park, a hike in the woods, or a day at the beach. These experiences foster physical activity, exploration, and an appreciation for the world beyond screens.

As we embark on the journey of digital well-being, this chapter reminds us that it's not about demonizing screens or rejecting technology. It's about crafting a blueprint that honors both our digital natives' curiosity and their well-being. By embracing a balanced digital lifestyle, we equip our children to thrive in a world that seamlessly blends the virtual and the real—a world where digital well-being is a cornerstone of a fulfilled, healthy life.

Cyber Bullying Awareness: Safeguarding Children From Online Threats

In the sprawling landscape of the digital age, where connection and communication transcend physical boundaries, the issue of cyber bullying has emerged as a poignant challenge for children and their guardians alike. The chapter on "Cyber bullying Awareness: Safeguarding Children from Online Threats" within the "Tech-Smart Parenting Toolkit" delves into the intricate realm of digital interactions, empowering parents with knowledge and strategies to shield their digital natives from the shadows of online harassment.

The Digital Playground: A New Frontier of Bullying:
As children explore the virtual playground, they encounter a new form of bullying that transcends physical boundaries. Cyber bullying takes many forms—from hurtful messages to spreading rumors—and can inflict deep emotional wounds. This chapter unveils the various manifestations of cyber bullying, enabling parents to recognize its nuances.

Understanding the Impact: Emotional and Psychological Toll:
Cyber bullying is not just confined to screens; its impact resonates deeply in the hearts and minds of its victims. This chapter delves into the emotional and psychological toll that cyber bullying can inflict, emphasizing the importance of fostering open lines of communication to ensure children feel comfortable discussing their experiences.

Prevention: The First Line of Defense:

Prevention is a powerful tool in the fight against cyber bullying. This chapter equips parents with proactive strategies to prevent cyber bullying incidents, such as educating children about responsible online behavior, setting privacy settings, and guiding them on who to connect with in the digital world.

Recognizing Warning Signs: Navigating the Unseen:

Sometimes, the signs of cyber bullying may not be readily apparent. Changes in behavior, mood swings, and reluctance to engage in digital activities are subtle indicators that warrant attention. This chapter provides insights into recognizing these warning signs, enabling parents to address potential issues before they escalate.

Communication: A Shield Against Cyber bullying:

An open channel of communication is a potent shield against cyber bullying. This chapter emphasizes the significance of creating an environment where children feel safe sharing their digital experiences. By nurturing a trusting relationship, parents can offer support and guidance when faced with cyber bullying situations.

Addressing Cyber bullying: Empowering Children to Respond:

When cyber bullying occurs, children need guidance on how to respond effectively. This chapter offers strategies for children to assert themselves, report incidents to trusted adults, and seek help from appropriate sources. Empowering children with tools to navigate such situations instills a sense of agency and resilience.

Seeking Help: Partnering with Schools and Authorities:

Cyber bullying often extends beyond home boundaries. Schools and authorities play a crucial role in addressing these issues. This chapter guides parents on collaborating with educational institutions and law enforcement to ensure a comprehensive approach to addressing cyber bullying incidents.

Digital Empathy and Kindness: Nurturing Positive Online Interactions:

Preventing cyber bullying is not only about avoiding negative behavior; it's also about promoting positive digital interactions. This chapter emphasizes the value of digital empathy and kindness, encouraging parents to instill these virtues in their children's online interactions.

Conclusion: Navigating the Digital Frontier Together:

As technology continues to evolve, so does the realm of cyber bullying. This chapter concludes by emphasizing the importance of ongoing vigilance and communication. By remaining informed, engaged, and empathetic, parents can create a digital fortress that protects their children from the perils of cyber bullying, ensuring that their digital journeys are marked by positivity, resilience, and empowerment.

Fostering Digital Citizenship: Instilling Responsible Digital Behavior

In the vast and interconnected landscape of the digital world, the concept of digital citizenship has emerged as a guiding light, illuminating the path toward responsible and ethical behavior. The chapter on "Fostering Digital Citizenship: Instilling Responsible Digital Behavior" within the "Tech-Smart Parenting Toolkit" delves into the heart of this concept, equipping parents with the tools and insights needed to cultivate a generation of digital citizens who navigate the online realm with integrity and mindfulness.

The New Frontier of Citizenship:

As the digital age reshapes the boundaries of our interactions, the definition of citizenship has expanded to encompass the virtual spaces we inhabit. This chapter initiates an exploration into the essence of digital citizenship—a concept rooted in respect, empathy, and ethical conduct.

Understanding the Digital Footprint: Impact and Consequences:
The digital footprints we leave behind are like echoes in the virtual corridors. This chapter delves into the concept of a digital footprint, highlighting how every click, share, and post contributes to a digital legacy. Understanding the impact and potential consequences of our actions is the first step toward responsible digital behavior.

Navigating the Ethical Maze: Teachable Moments in Technology:
From copyright considerations to responsible content sharing, the digital realm is fraught with ethical nuances. This chapter guides parents in recognizing and capitalizing on teachable moments—opportunities to discuss and model ethical decision-making in the digital context.

Promoting Respectful Online Interactions: The Power of Empathy:
Empathy, a cornerstone of good citizenship, extends into the digital realm. This chapter explores how parents can foster empathetic online interactions by encouraging children to consider the feelings and perspectives of others, leading to a more harmonious online environment.

Combatting Cyber bullying: A Call for Digital Advocacy:
In the battle against cyber bullying, digital citizenship stands as a stalwart defender. This chapter discusses strategies for combatting cyber bullying through digital advocacy—empowering children to stand up against negativity and injustice in the online sphere.

Media Literacy: Navigating the Sea of Information:
In the era of information overload, discernment is paramount. This chapter underscores the importance of media literacy, helping children navigate the sea of information, critically evaluate sources, and form informed opinions.

Balancing Online and Offline Lives: A Lesson in Digital Equilibrium:
Digital citizenship isn't just about online behavior; it's about striking a balance between the virtual and the real. This chapter delves into the art of

maintaining a healthy equilibrium, where technology enriches rather than dominates our lives.

Responsible Content Creation: Cultivating a Positive Digital Presence:
The digital world offers a platform for creative expression. This chapter guides parents in helping their children create content that reflects their authentic selves and contributes positively to the digital community.

As the chapter draws to a close, it underscores the significance of digital citizenship as a foundation for cultivating responsible leaders in the digital landscape. By nurturing digital citizens who practice empathy, integrity, and ethical conduct, parents pave the way for a generation that not only navigates the online world with grace but also contributes to its growth and evolution.

Conclusion

In the captivating journey we've embarked upon through the pages of "Tech-Smart Generation: Empowering Digital Natives," we've unraveled the intricate tapestry of modern education and parenting in the digital era. As we approach the culmination of this enlightening voyage, let us reflect on the profound insights we've gathered and the transformative potential that lies within our grasp.

In a world where technology evolves at a breathtaking pace, our digital natives stand at the threshold of unprecedented opportunities and challenges. This book has been a compass, guiding us through the dynamic landscape of education, teaching, and parenting in the digital age. From the Tech-Smart School Kits to the Tech-Smart Teaching Kits, and finally, to the Tech-Smart Parenting Kits, each volume holds a unique treasure trove of strategies, insights, and tools that empower us to navigate this digital frontier with confidence and wisdom.

As we conclude this volume, remember that the power to shape the future rests in our hands. By immersing ourselves in the complete trilogy of Tech-Smart Kits, we are equipping ourselves to foster innovation, cultivate digital fluency, and nurture responsible digital citizenship in the lives of our children. The comprehensive wisdom within these pages illuminates pathways to success for the generation poised to redefine the world.

So, dear reader, I invite you to embark on this holistic journey of empowerment. Dive into the Complete Books; 1."Tech-Smart School Kits: Practical Strategies for

Empowering Digital Natives" *to revolutionize educational paradigms, explore the 2.* ***"Tech-Smart Teaching Kits: Practical Strategies for Nurturing Digital Natives"*** *to harness the full potential of technology in the classroom, and delve into the 3.* ***"Tech-Smart Parenting Kits: Practical Strategies for Raising Digital Natives"*** *to cultivate a harmonious digital environment at home.*

The voyage we undertake isn't just about embracing the digital age; it's about steering its course. As educators, parents, and guardians, our collective commitment to fostering a Tech-Smart Generation is a testament to our dedication to nurturing future leaders, innovators, and citizens who will thrive in an ever-evolving world.

So, let us continue to explore, learn, and adapt—armed with the insights within these three volumes—to create a legacy of empowered digital natives who will not only conquer the challenges of the digital landscape but also shape its destiny. The journey beckons, and the rewards are boundless. Let us step forward with purpose and embrace the extraordinary potential that lies ahead.

Acknowledgments

The culmination of the Tech-Smart Trilogy—comprising the Tech-Smart School Toolkit, Tech-Smart Teaching Toolkit, and Tech-Smart Parenting Toolkit—stands as a collaborative endeavor, woven together by the threads of numerous individuals and organizations whose contributions and support have been nothing short of invaluable. We extend our sincere appreciation to the diverse tapestry of collaborators who have breathed life into this ambitious project.

Foremost, we wish to express our heartfelt gratitude to the educators, administrators, and mentors whose steadfast dedication to advancing education through technology has formed the bedrock of this trilogy. Your insights, experiences, and innovative approaches have infused these pages with profound wisdom and practicality.

Our heartfelt appreciation extends to our circle of colleagues, friends, and family whose encouragement, constructive feedback, and constant inspiration have been the wind beneath our wings. Your unwavering belief in the transformative power of technology in education has been the driving force propelling us forward on this journey.

A resounding acknowledgment is due to the educational institutions that graciously opened their doors, inviting us to immerse ourselves in their tech-smart environments. Your willingness to share your experiences has provided us with a canvas upon which to observe, learn, and collaborate. Your commitment to fostering innovation has been a guiding light throughout this expedition.

Lastly, we extend our heartfelt thanks to the readers of these books—the trailblazers of the digital revolution in education. Your eagerness to embrace new frontiers and navigate the ever-evolving technological landscape fuels our dedication to exploring novel pathways that empower learners.

The Tech-Smart Trilogy stands as a testament to the collective spirit and unwavering commitment of all who champion the potential of technology to enrich and revolutionize the learning experiences of digital natives. Each thread you've woven into this tapestry is integral to its strength and beauty.

With profound gratitude,

Pere C. Fufeyin.

About The Author

Pere C. Fufeyin, the visionary mind behind the groundbreaking trilogy of books, stands as an eminent educator who has dedicated over two decades to shaping the future of education in a tech-centric world. At the core of this trilogy is Pere's unwavering passion for harnessing technology's potential to empower both educators and students.

In the "Tech-Smart Teaching Toolkit," Pere's expertise shines through as he seamlessly bridges the gap between traditional teaching methods and the demands of digital natives. This toolkit serves as a guiding compass, offering educators actionable strategies to navigate the ever-evolving digital landscape while fostering engagement and critical thinking.

Moving through the trilogy, the "Tech-Smart School Kits" illuminate a pathway for educational institutions to integrate technology seamlessly into their environments. The "Tech-Smart Teaching Kits" delve into the heart of pedagogy, equipping educators with the finesse to wield digital tools effectively while tailoring learning experiences to individual needs.

The trilogy culminates with the "Tech-Smart Parenting Kits," addressing the pivotal role of parents in guiding their children's digital journeys. Pere's insights empower parents to nurture responsible digital citizens, striking equilibrium between online exploration and offline growth.

As technology continues to shape the way we learn, teach, and live, Pere's trilogy stands as a testament to his commitment to revolutionizing education. With each kit, educators, parents, and institutions are armed with the knowledge and tools necessary to cultivate a generation prepared to thrive in the digitally driven future.

ORDER COPIES OF THE TECH-SMART TRILOGY NOW

Tech-Smart School Toolkit: Practical Strategies for Empowering Digital Natives.

Tech-Smart Teaching Toolkit: Practical Strategies for Nurturing Digital Natives.

Tech-Smart Parenting Toolkit: Practical Strategies for Raising Digital Natives.